The Raccoon Whisperer The Story of James Blackwood

By Christine MacKinnon

Also by Christine MacKinnon

Chronicles from the Hall

This book is dedicated to the memory of Jim's father, Cecil Blackwood

And to the memory of my mother, Rita (Mahoney) Richards

# FORWARD

I happily admit that I have become addicted to being lulled to sleep by the sounds of raccoons eating grapes. Even in this statement, however, I am not being fully truthful as the sound is only mesmerizing when it is coupled with the visual of raccoons tilting their heads back as not to waste a single drop of each grape's sweet juice. It's quite comical to watch. Buddy and the gang are simply doing what raccoons do, and I've got a front- row seat that offers more intimacy than most zoos. It almost feels as though I am intruding on a family's private mealtime, yet the images are so captivating that I'm unable to tear myself away. I, along with so many others, feel more than fortunate to be on the receiving end of this daily gift. These mealtime videos calm the anxious, provide cheer to the sad, and allow the entire world to reconsider their opinions of raccoons.

James Blackwood is the mastermind behind these treasured videos, yet he would never consider himself to be anything more than an ordinary guy, It's likely, his humility that makes him so endearing. His first video posted on YouTube is dated July 1, 2011, which means that he has been sharing this part of his life and himself for nearly ten years. It is more than impressive because he was not making the videos for anybody's benefit other than his own. However, when the world found itself fighting a global pandemic amidst social unrest during the summer of 2020, I found myself scouring YouTube for anything that could offer me a peaceful and quiet moment. YouTube must know me well because when the algorithms suggested a video post from someone called RACCOON WHISPERER, I took the bait.

I can still recall the very first video that I watched that summer. My jaw was dragging on the floor. I literally could not believe what my eyes were seeing. Yes, I'm a country girl from rural North Carolina, but I grew up knowing that there were just some animals that we were to keep our distance from— raccoons were among them. I knew them to be fierce, rabid wild animals that might attack any human that looked at them inappropriately. So how in the heck was this man sitting on his patio being friendly with not one but well over 10 of them? For the life of me, I could not wrap my head around it. Why wasn't he wearing any protective gear? How was he able to be so calm? And in the name of everything holy, what was possessing these wild animals to patiently wait their turn for their next piece of hot dog? In that moment I had no answers to any of these questions, and I must have stayed awake until about 3:00 am watching one video after another from this RACCOON WHISPERER looking for any answer that made sense.

Through the series of videos that I watched that night, these are the things that I have learned about Mr. Blackwood.

He is a gentle giant.
He is a lover of animals, He is a humanitarian.
He is kindness personified.
He is the epitome of generosity. He enjoys the simple things in life.
He loves Connor Cat and Charlotte. He is a decent human being.
He misses and loves his late wife.
He lives by an honourable moral code. He loves to laugh.
He hates to see his fur babies in pain.

As a therapist, I hate to see humans in pain. Over the coming weeks as I continued to watch these cheerful videos, every now and then I would venture to the comments—curious to see if others were having similar reactions to my own. Unsurprisingly, most were. However, in true internet fashion even this kind, sweet, dear man had trolls. There were individuals that called Mr. Blackwood names. Some had opinions about the cleanliness of the raccoon's drinking water (they are wild animals, mind you). Others had thoughts about the diet that he provided them. After having had enough of the ridiculous comments, I wrote a letter to Mr. Blackwood offering some words of encouragement. Given the size of his viewership, I didn't anticipate that he would read the letter right away, and I certainly never expected a response. I was wrong on both counts, and the unlikely friendship that blossomed over the next several months taught me even more about this exceptional human being. Much of it, you too, will learn as Christine has done a lovely job of letting you into his life. I know you'll come to love and appreciate Jim just as much as I do.

He is more than a YouTuber.
He is a man I am thrilled to call FRIEND. He is Jim Blackwood, and
He is our RACCOON WHISPERER.

Dr. Jaz Robbins Artist/Author/Adjunct Professor
Pepperdine University Malibu, California

# INTRODUCTION

The world of Jim Blackwood and his life as The Raccoon Whisperer was first introduced to me by a friend back in September of 2020. The world was in the middle of a pandemic and I, like many others, was pretty much housebound. Shopping, travelling, and any kind of social gatherings was just a dream. My friend has known Jim for many years and suggested that I check out one of his many YouTube videos. At the time, Jim had approximately 80,000 followers but the number was quickly growing. I'll be honest here and say that I knew next to nothing about raccoons or, indeed, about Jim. I frankly couldn't understand the appeal of watching the little creatures eating, squabbling, or his obvious rapport with the little animals. A writer, by nature, has a curious soul, and I, no less than others, was fascinated by his growing popularity. I learned more about his life, both past and present, and quickly became enraptured. Reading through the thousands of comments by his loyal fans of many years, it quickly became obvious that he is making a huge difference in many lives.

He presents an air of kindness, authenticity, and a true love for his little furry friends. This, along with many of his other attributes, appeals to people of all ages. Jim somehow relaxes people, relieves their anxiety, calms children, puts others to sleep with the sweet sound of the raccoons eating their grapes– a sound that is remarkably like that of raindrops falling on a tin roof. He is undoubtedly genuine in his love for his followers and his animals.

An almost unbelievable thing happened on the night of Tuesday, November 3rd, 2020. After posting videos for more than 11 years, Jim uploaded one entitled MOBBED BY RACCOONS. The video went viral and attracted over 26 million views. That number rises daily. From that day on, the world of THE RACCOON WHISPERER was launched into the stratosphere. He often gains anywhere from one to two to three thousand followers a day and has now got a following in the high six figures and a fan club of over 150,000 members.

CHAPTER ONE
YOUTUBE

YouTube is a form of social media that a person subscribes to by simply downloading an app designated by the now-famous white icon with the red right-facing arrow. In the past 15 years, many contributors have come and gone but YouTube has also produced a new generation of celebrities and influencers who have turned short videos into lucrative careers.

YouTube has become the launchpad for comedians, musicians gamers, and make-up artists/manufacturers by building up their subscriber base and in turn, has made many of them very rich indeed. We will forget famous musicians, record labels, and game manufacturers and instead focus on the ordinary people who have built a solid connection with their fan base and whose numbers are mind-boggling.

Multi-national channels in almost every language have made this a world that crosses all barriers, all cultures, all religious and all political views.

Many channels geared to children are particularly popular. One group known as LOS POLINENOS has 23.4 million subscribers, a figure that a major television network can only dream of for any given program.

A US gamer that goes by the name of NINJA has 23.9 million subscribers. He rose to fame but has now left YouTube for an exclusive deal with MICROSOFT MIXER SERVICE for an unknown, but obviously astronomical sum of money. His high energy and controversial commentary have been the key to his success.

Perhaps the most surprising star of all is a young nine-year-old boy named Ryan Kaji. He reviews toys, shows his experience playing with them and in turn made upwards of 22 million dollars in a single year. His channel is managed by his father and Ryan's appeal to the five to 12-year-old market is unprecedented. What child doesn't want to live vicariously through another while watching him or her playing with toys that they can only dream of owning? His videos also have more sophisticated content with links to his favourite TV shows, cartoons and books. His reviews are as real and honest as only a nine-year-olds' can be. Often the fate of a particular toy and its further distribution lays firmly in his hands. If Ryan loves it then sales skyrocket along with his earnings and his viewership. According to FORBES MAGAZINE, he is now the highest-paid contributor on YouTube.

A person can travel the world with vloggers, watch a gallbladder surgery, learn helpful tips and tricks from a licensed chiropractor, learn to bake bread, follow the finer points of assembling a particular brand of BBQ, learn to apply winged eyeliner, how to house train one's puppy and virtually millions of other lessons or forms of entertainment that lay in between.

There are over 37 million YouTube channels with the numbers growing. More than 23% upload over 500 million hours of video every minute of every day. The breadth and scope of this media form are endless.

I fell into the rabbit hole of YouTube about 10 years ago. Late at night and unable to sleep, I would listen to one make-up artist or another talking about application and tricks of the trade. I found, for the most part, their voices soothing and an excellent and much healthier alternative to a sleeping pill. Now I listen to videos by ASMR artists whose sole purpose is to lull one into a restful sleep. Nowadays, YouTube is my go-to place for answers to all sorts of issues from recipes, to health concerns, to the wonders of apple cider vinegar.

Actors bury their own personalities to become that of another. I believe that the key to Jim's success and to others who have become YouTube stars is to be oneself – no pretence – just a "what you see is what you get" attitude. He hides behind nothing, unless occasionally, it is the rear end of a raccoon. There is no showing off. He talks mostly to the raccoons and who of us, after all, needs to show off for an animal? We, his viewers, are onlookers into his raccoon world and are made to feel privileged if a comment is aimed directly at the camera, and therefore, feel like a friend and an important part of his world. There is no show of grandiosity, no tricks or fakery, just a kind, simple man. His authenticity comes across loud and clear to his followers. Many of his viewers are children and who more so than a child can spot a phoney, even over the airwaves.

Thumbnails are often said to be the key to drawing a person into one's channel. A potential viewer, upon opening the YouTube app is confronted with a number of small pictures designed to appeal to the eye. These photos or thumbnails can make or break a channel. First impressions are everything on YouTube. In this fast-moving world, a person has just seconds to make an impression. A lot of successful channels use professional thumbnail designers to view each video and come up with the best shot to capture a potential audience. Jim has never used the skills of such a person. He chooses his own shots and so far they've never failed. He's had some very pushy designers call to sell him their expertise but it's obvious that he's doing just fine on his own. They make promises to double his viewership, however, Jim's personal thumbnails have grown his channel by more than 300%. He's also had offers from manufacturers offering to do RACCOON WHISPERER merchandise. So far he's turned down all such offers.

To know more about the YouTube phenomenon that is James Blackwood, THE RACCOON WHISPERER, let's go back to his beginnings.

CHAPTER TWO
THE BEGINNING

This is an ordinary story about an ordinary man, who through no intent or wish of his own, has reached extraordinary heights.

Jim was born on Hoyt Street in a small town in Northern Nova Scotia, Canada, called Westville. The residents of the small town primarily eked out their living from the many seams of coal that run, like the capillaries of the human body, underground and extending for many miles. After a disaster (preceded by many other disasters), in 1992, the mines shut down for good. Close to the larger town of New Glasgow, many of the county's residents also worked for the then Scott Paper Mill or the Michelin Tire Factory, both of which were thriving industries in the 1960s and 1970s. All that is left now is Michelin Tire. The closure of both the paper mill and the mines left the residents of Pictou County struggling. Many left for the riches of the oil fields of Alberta. But just like many towns dependant on singular enterprises, recovery is not an option. People go on and eventually thrive once again.

Jim was a child of the 50s and 60s, the youngest of four children and the only boy, born to Cecil and Kathleen Blackwood. He had a humble beginning with a father who made his living as a bus driver and a mother who took in sewing to make ends meet. Both lived well into their old age and Jim loved them both dearly. He dedicates this book to the memory of his dad who was the single greatest influence in his life. To this day, he says that the most difficult thing he has ever done was to give his father's eulogy. His father's simple acts of kindness impacted the lives of all who rode his regular bus route everyday. Jim strives to measure up to the example that his father set for him. After reading this book I think that you'll agree – Jim has lived up to and even surpassed those standards. I have no doubt that his father smiles down on him from heaven every day.

He spent most of his childhood as did many of his generation playing road hockey, skating on frozen ponds, sledding, and throwing a ball in the fields every summer. In other words, a childhood spent mostly out of doors in the fresh air. Television was then only entering the households of the wealthy and privileged. These were the days before children were slaves to a screen of any kind. Jim moved to the nearby town of Stellarton at the age of eight. Parents, grandparents, siblings and aunts and uncles inhabited the same house making for a close-knit family unit.

With the blind, impetuous vigor of youth, his passion, from the age of four or so, after receiving a toy airplane from Santa, became flying and aircraft of any description. His ambition from that early age was to become a pilot. In his teen years, when not working at the local Pepsi bottling plant, he became an Air Cadet for six years with the single-minded ambition of using it as a stepping stone into the Royal Canadian Air Force. As a grown man and up until a few years ago, he owned a flight simulator, valued at about $5,000. He decided to sell it when he came to the realization that he was spending every waking moment on it and was well and truly addicted.

Jim graduated from high school but decided that his future lay in the cockpit of a fighter jet and not college or university. As a teenager, he also became a self-taught musician, proficient in playing both the piano and drums and even ventured into singing. After the insurrection at The Capital Building in Washington, D.C. in early January of 2021, Jim took to his brand new keyboard to play THE STAR SPANGLED BANNER, solely by ear, as a special tribute to his many fans in the United States. According to the comments on his video that night he brought many to tears because of his thoughtfulness. Their gratitude was boundless.

He later took a computer course at a community college and found that he had a natural gift for all forms of technology. He proudly says that there isn't a device that he can't repair and has never had to use the services of an expert because he is the expert.

His first heartbreak came when his application for the Air Force was turned down. No reason was given for this denial. He heard that the RCMP was looking for recruits and the dream of wearing one uniform became the dream of wearing another. He was accepted into The Royal Canadian Mounted Police Training Academy in Regina almost immediately. The RCMP is the federal policing agency of Canada. It is and was a great honor to become a member of this elite police force and his family and most especially his father was very proud. Just months into his training he received word from the Air Force that there had been a mistake. Jim was never privy to what that mistake was and his application was now accepted. Welcome to The Royal Canadian Air Force!

"Too late," he told them. "I'm about to graduate from the RCMP."

I expect that they lived to regret their error.

At six feet tall and with shoulders so broad that all uniform components had to be tailored to fit, he cut a fine figure in that stunning red serge jacket, jodhpurs, stetson, and tall leather boots, a uniform known throughout the world. His pride is evident in photos taken on the steps of the academy at his graduation ceremonies. He was just 19 years old.

His first posting was to Newfoundland, an island just 90 miles off the coast of Nova Scotia, and the last province to join the Dominion of Canada. It is the most easterly point of North America and played a strategic role during World War II. To Jim, Newfoundland might just as well have been a million miles away. It is still only accessible by a lengthy ferry ride or by air. Jim would no longer be able to drop by to see his parents for special family events and most definitely not be able to afford a plane ticket home on a regular basis. Even now Jim is not much of a traveller, preferring instead the comforts of home and the company of his animal friends. At present, he doesn't even possess a passport.

Jim's first posting was to a small town called Grand Bank on the island's southern shore. It was not unlike the one in which he grew up. Jim spent a year there, two years in St. John's, the province's capital, and then on to Clarenville followed by a further two years in an even smaller town farther west, called Wesleyville. Nowadays, transfers amongst members of the RCMP occur less often. The stress of such frequent moving about did not make for efficient policing. It was during Jim's time in Clarenville that an event occurred that made Constable Jim Blackwood a household name with repercussions that would follow him for the rest of his days.

## CHAPTER THREE
## THE SIGHTING

In the early morning hours of October 26th, 1978 at approximately 1:50 am, Constable Blackwood took his partner home and proceeded back to the detachment to drop off his RCMP cruiser at the end of his shift. Once there he received a call from a resident located nearby who reported seeing an unusual object hovering in the sky above. Jim immediately drove to the spot where he met a gentleman who was accompanied by some of his family members. The 40-year-old man and the other onlookers were obviously lucid and sober. Upon arrival, the caller immediately handed Jim his binoculars to better observe the object hovering in the night sky. Jim looked through the binoculars to see an unusual shape moving slowly from west to east at an altitude of somewhere between 2,000-3,000 feet. The craft, at this point, was just ½ mile from Clarenville above the northeast coast of Random Islands. With the naked eye, Jim could see blue flashing lights that blinked far more rapidly than any that he'd ever seen on any ordinary aircraft. Jim was an avid aviation enthusiast and there wasn't any aircraft manufactured by man that he couldn't identify. He had studied the locations of all lighting, speed, altitudes and entrances and exits of every plane imaginable. After all, it had been his passion from the time that he was four years old. The originators of this "flight" could not have picked a better witness to their visit.

After a few moments of observation, he returned to the detachment to obtain the RCMP's 15X to 60X resolution telescope. It was far and away a much more powerful tool to see the object that was floating in the cloudless night sky. With this device, the sight above was truly astonishing. Jim observed more clearly now, the blue flashing lights which appeared to be emanating from both sides accompanied by another red flashing light on the top of the craft. Obviously taken aback by the sight, he zoomed in to see something that completely filled the lens of the telescope. The bottom third of the craft was now completely aglow with no obvious source, the light so bright that it was nearly blinding.

None of the lights appeared to have any socket source and did not protrude in any way. They were just there. It was at this point that Jim put on the emergency light bar on the top of his police cruiser. This is where things got even stranger. The lights of the craft started to flash as if in response. They flashed more rapidly than any light source that Jim had ever been confronted with before. He likened them to the strobe lights often used by rock bands of the time. The object then turned and showed its other side, When Jim zeroed in on the lighting system a little closer he was able to observe that the top red light had now changed to a flashing sequence that went back and forth between red and white.

To Jim's eyes, and to that of the other observers that were present, the object was oval-shaped with a very small tail, pointed "nose" that could not possibly be of any service to a regular aircraft. Stranger still, it made no sound at all. He estimated it to be between 30-40 feet long and to Jim, it appeared to be beyond the present understanding of modern-day aerodynamics. A simple drawing of the craft, sketched by Jim later that night, reminds me of a large whale of some sort. But this was definitely not a sea creature. None known to man could possibly operate with such a small "tail" nor obviously hover in the night sky.

After 1½ hours the craft began to turn and raise itself up and down at a very low rate of speed. One can only wonder if it was the long goodbye because right after that, it flew off, with no warm-up or warning, faster than the speed of a jet. By this time Jim had returned to the detachment and was able to fully view its departure. In a split second, it completely disappeared from sight. Jim, immediately and prudently viewed some nearby stars and quickly ascertained that none were nearly close enough to be observed in the way that he could observe this craft.

In later interviews and his police report, Jim likened the size as somewhere between a 737 and a DC8. The craft had no visible doors or windows of any kind and no markings to signify its origin or call letters. It seemed to Jim that the object was extremely heavy, a perception made because of his vast knowledge of aircraft and their construction.

The eyewitness testified to the fact that he had seen the craft in the night sky a week before as did a media source who wished to remain anonymous. He also agreed with Jim's observations that the object seemed to be constructed of a very dull metallic fabrication that Jim had never seen in all his years of aircraft studies.

Fully aware that most people did not or could not believe in UFO sightings, he understood why many were reluctant to report such events. Things are no different now than they were in 1978.

He called in his Sargent who helped him to write a report on the incident which would no doubt be considered controversial by anybody's standards. The report was then locked in the detachment's safe and dispatched to the Commissioner of the RCMP in Ottawa later that day.

In further television interviews, it's obvious, without a shadow of a doubt, that the report was made in a clear and concise manner worthy of an excellent police officer with amazing observational skills. There could be no question of his sincerity or honesty.

Word spread quickly of the UFO sighting and so did the good-natured jokes and ribbing thrown at Jim from his fellow officers. There was no doubt in their minds that what he said was the truth as he knew it. He was called Mork from Ork and humorous drawings appeared on the office bulletin board of strange-looking aliens calling his name from flying saucers.

But the notoriety didn't end there. NTV, the local affiliate of Canada's top media outlet interviewed Jim at length. In his uniform, he appeared authentic and completely believable. Jim admitted to me that during the interview, he was being mocked by his colleagues who were looking in through a window – making faces, thumbs in ears with wiggling tongues protruding. Those who had the ability stuck out their false teeth. But through it all Jim remained composed and professional. Soon, he was giving interviews to television, newspapers and radio stations from all over the world. After all, this was not some crackpot drunk on a highway in the middle of the night. This was a well-respected member of one of the most respected police forces in the world.

He was interviewed by MUFON, the official investigators of all documented UFO sightings in the world. Once his police report went to Ottawa, The National Research Council became involved and formally said that they didn't believe him. Informally, one can only surmise that they just wanted to shut him up about the events of that night. In 2016, there was a similar documented sighting in the very same location where Jim had his encounter. It's difficult to say how many there may have been between 1978 and 2016. People don't expect to be believed so they keep quiet and don't report their experiences.

The little town of Clarenville was now on the international map and did its best to capitalize on the sighting. Jim's hockey team officially changed their name to the CLARENVILLE UFO'S. The local Holiday Inn offered a weekend package for two. The deal was, undoubtedly, taken advantage of by many members of the international media and those who regularly follow reported sightings all over the world.

On October 16, 2020, The Canadian Mint issued a series of three coins to commemorate three well-documented sightings of UFOs in Canada. The first sighting occurred in Shag Harbour, Nova Scotia, on October 4, 1967, the second in Falcon Lake, Manitoba on May 29, 1967, and the third was the sighting in Clarenville, Newfoundland. The coins were sold out in just 10 days. They have a face value of $20.00 but because only a limited number were released, their value on eBay and other such sites is quickly rising. The coin was sold with a black light that allows it to glow in the dark, making it a remarkable purchase for any collector. A visit to The Canadian Mint website gives a full description of all the sightings. Jim was awarded three of these coins free of charge.

Having never taken the time to think about any alien life form before that night in 1978, Jim believes that it would be naive to think that we are alone in the universe. Astronomers are regularly discovering new stars and new galaxies that revolve around other parts of the universe.

CHAPTER FOUR
THE LIGHTER SIDE OF POLICING

Perhaps the most significant event in the life of Jim, apart from his career, occurred shortly after his arrival in Clarenville. It was there that he met a girl, fell in love, and married her at the tender age of 23. His wife was just 17. As so often happens in marriages between two people of such a young age the marriage was short-lived. Having a partner in the police force is a challenge under any circumstances. It's not uncommon for a young woman to fall in love with the uniform. There's a phenomenon known amongst officers called Scarlet Fever, an obvious reference to the striking red dress uniform of the RCMP. A young handsome Mountie with a steady income was an attractive prospect during the challenging days of the then flailing Newfoundland economy. But a young woman, unused to the difficult demands and worry of sending a husband off every day into any manner of danger can be difficult to cope with. The marriage, unfortunately, did not last. But the bright spot was the birth of a son, Jim's only child. Another outcome of the divorce was that his wife moved on. We all know that a new man on the scene can come between a birth father and his relationship with his child. An estrangement was inevitable and sadly lasts until this day. The eventual and happy outcome, though, was the birth of a grandson, Gavin, born twelve years ago. Both grandfather and grandson are now the light of each other's life. His grandson became aware of his Poppy's videos and soon an unbreakable bond developed between the two. They FaceTime regularly and his grandson has proudly dubbed him Poppy Raccoon. A recent picture shows him to be a miniature of Jim at the same age.

Jim's early days in Newfoundland, and indeed, in every posting that he had, meant dealing with some discomforts that he and other officers had to bear. Single officers were required to stay in barracks attached to the station for months at a time. The barracks were often in close proximity to the offices and the cells. One can only imagine the relentless clatter from the old Remington typewriters, the constant barrage of noises from the teletype machines, the yelling from one office to another across hallways, the ramblings of a drunk in a nearby cell, or the pounding of those knee-high leather boots accompanied by the clinking of the attached spurs. The noise went on all day, every day while an off-duty officer tried to sleep after a night shift. He was often required to shave and use the facilities in a cell right beside a prisoner. Sleeplessness was the norm. A regular day or night required an officer to drive approximately 300-400 miles and burn at least two tanks of gasoline during any given shift. Newfoundland, despite its large geographical size, is sparsely populated in and around the outport communities, which are often many miles apart. An officer's jurisdiction can span over many hundreds of miles.

Sometimes Jim even had to sleep in a cell. Sometimes they were empty. Sometimes they were not. Jim would be forced to take the prisoners for bathroom breaks or listen to their drunken conversations for hours on end, all the while trying to get a few hours of sleep in between.

Even with his months of training in Regina, Jim refers to those early days in the force as his "baptism by fire." The fact that Newfoundland had just 30 years before been a part of the British Empire meant that all statutes of the Criminal Code had not caught up to the rest of Canada. As a member of the RCMP, an officer had to prosecute their own cases before a magistrate even if the opposing side had a lawyer. It was obviously a huge learning curve for any officer.

Jim lost his first case because he could not establish jurisdiction when a witness failed to relay where the offence occurred. He never again repeated the same mistake. If the Department of Fisheries was prosecuting, (Grand Bank was a fishing community), they often had a government lawyer to handle the case for them. Jim stood up to the best of them and never lost. Grand Bank, being as isolated as it was, often meant that the lawyer couldn't make it into town. Jim or a fellow officer would step in to take the case. He became adept at prosecuting and learned more about the criminal code during those times than he had in Regina at the training academy. In larger areas, like St. John's, where Jim was later stationed, some officers did nothing but prosecute every day in court. While policing in Clarenville, Jim and his fellow officers would take the job in turn, on a monthly basis. Unfortunately, they were not paid as well as any lawyer.

When Jim arrived in Grand Bank he did not have any training as a supervisor but because of the shortage in manpower, he did many jobs that were well above his pay grade. One of these jobs was that of a Driver's

Licence Examiner for the province. Driver training was a big part of the education at the academy and he did have the qualifications to do the job. He just never expected that he'd have to be an examiner. His very first test was with an elderly lady who was applying for a licence renewal. Another man was to be tested on the same day. It was quiet in the office so Jim's Corporal said that he should take the lady and the Corporal would take the man.

Off they went in separate directions. A total of five mistakes was the difference between a driver being granted or denied the right to drive. There was, of course, a checklist in place. Pulling up to one of the few intersects in the small town, the lady got confused, pulled out into the oncoming traffic, and proceeded to strike the vehicle coming from the other direction. The car that she hit carried the Corporal and his applicant. Both drivers failed and both officers were required to fill out an accident report that was then submitted to head office. One can only imagine the laughter that ensued from their Commanders.

When Jim was first transferred to St. John's he was assigned to desk duty for a while, answering phones, radios, registering firearms ad doing the brutal job of driver's examinations. This time the lady took him down a dead-end street. Jim obviously didn't know the city well so he had no way of predicting where he was going to end up. He instructed the driver to back up so they could exit the street.

Whereupon she informed him, "I'm sorry officer, but I don't do reverse."

Jim took over the wheel at this point, backed the car into a driveway and they proceeded on their way. Needless to say, Jim did not ask her to show her skills at parallel parking. He did, however, have to rely on her instructions to find his way back to the detachment, Unfortunately, she didn't know that information either, assuming that he did. He had to knock on the door of a nearby house (Police officers are very reluctant to do this except in the case of a dire emergency) to call for a squad car to escort them back to the station. A fail for her and much ribbing from his colleagues for Jim.

Underwear theft seems to be a big problem for police everywhere but none more so than in Newfoundland where it is still the norm for people to hang their clothes on the line outside. The most egregious of these incidents was perpetrated on a single mother with one child. She came to the detachment to make a report saying that she and her child were forced to go "commando" because they had absolutely no underwear left at all. Constable Jim and others dipped into petty cash and purchased some pieces, hung it on her line and waited for the thief to make his appearance. The bandit turned out to be a teenage boy, whom I suspect, after being caught red-handed by the RCMP, never committed such a crime again.

Another like-minded thief was caught after a trail of dropped panties led Jim and other officers on a trek through the woods to the bank of a nearby brook where he was apprehended with a pair of panties on his head and others strewn about his semi-naked person. One more successful arrest!

Back in the early 1970s, the Canadian Government sold what were called "Olympic Lottery Tickets." They were sold before the inception of the National Lottery and were in aid of contributing to the cost of The Olympics in Montreal, Quebec. The tickets could only be purchased at a registered banking institution. Each ticket cost $10.00. The grand prize was one million dollars. Jim was on traffic patrol and noticed an elderly gentleman on the highway just outside St. John's. The truck was in a sad state of disrepair. He pulled the truck over and saw that the pickup had bald tires, no rear lights, no horn, and dangerously compromised brakes. Jim could have written a ticket for each infraction but thought he would give the old guy a break and charge him, instead, with defective equipment. One $10 fine was much kinder than several $10 fines. Jim explained all this to the driver who was obviously very grateful.

The elderly man replied, "God bless you, my son. It's really kind of you to do that and if I wins anything on my ticket I'll be sure to split it with you."

Obviously not the worldly sort, the poor man thought that he was being given a lottery ticket.

On another warm summer evening while on patrol outside Clarenville, Jim found himself coming up to a fork in the road and following directly behind a driver who turned on his right signal light but turned left instead. Jim immediately activated his roof lights and pulled the driver over.

"Sir, why did you put on your right signal when you made a left-hand turn?"

The driver answered, "My left-hand signal doesn't work so I thought it best to make some kind of signal to show that I was turning somewhere."

The hand signal portion of his driver's manual had obviously been left unread.

In one of the detachments that Jim worked in, it was common practice to use retirees for jail guards. The jobs were almost always on a part-time basis. The guards ranged anywhere from 67-85 years of age. One little old man was quite an accomplished spoon player. For those unaware, spoons are just that—two spoons banged together to make music. It's an old Irish form of entertainment (Newfoundland is primarily made up of Irish immigrants who came over on boats during the potato famine or as prisoners). The spoons are likely a throw black to the day when musical instruments were expensive and hard to come by. It may sound unmelodic but when played well, the sound is quite lovely. It's still a big form of entertainment in a lot of small Scottish and Irish communities. This particular character took his musical abilities to a whole new level. He would play soda cans off the top of his little bald head. Strangely enough, he never missed a beat. It's hard to imagine what the sound would be like but Jim, with his knowledge of music, swears it was a talent not to be missed.

And then there's the case of the blind lookout man. A call came into the station about a suspected after-hours robbery at a hardware store. Jim arrived on the scene to find three men armed with soldering guns. It was clear to Jim, that their intent was to break into the safe. He was alone at the time, in his vehicle, one man of a two-man detachment. His police cruiser was parked outside directly in front of the hardware store and Jim was standing right behind the lookout man.

The three men said in unison to their comrade, "Thanks a lot for telling us the cops are here."

"Well bye's, ya knows I'm blind as a bat." All the while unknowing that Jim was behind him.

Jim cuffed them all together and he later told me that the propane torches that they were using wouldn't even generate enough heat to burn their hands let alone through an iron safe. The four men pleaded guilty but received no jail time. The judge threw the case out of court on the grounds of stupidity.

Many of the police cruisers in smaller communities were unfit for road duty. Jim was often assigned to drive an old Dodge Polaris for his 300-400 mile per night treks.  This particular car's brakes failed one night, and with Jim behind the wheel, ended up overturned in the woods and was then promptly written off.  Luckily, no harm came to Jim and no officer was sad to see its demise.

Another routine traffic stop ended rather strangely when Jim pulled over an elderly lady for speeding.  She immediately rolled down her window and grabbed Jim in a place on his body where no person has the right to touch another.  After his initial shock, he wrote her a ticket.  She apparently tried the same trick shortly afterward with another officer that ended with the same result.  She was charged and convicted of assaulting an officer.

While with the St. John's detachment, a break-in occurred at a local warehouse.  Items were missing so an officer and his canine partner were called in to track down the missing loot.  The dog was released into the woods behind the warehouse and returned some minutes later munching on a Crispy Crunch Bar.

"Oh, good doggy.  Now go find us the rest."  Off he went into the woods a second time and returned munching on another Crispy Crunch Bar.

After many attempts, the dog downright refused to show Jim and the dog handler where the rest of the stash was hidden.  The crime was eventually solved, the merchandise retrieved, but not with the help of the dog.

Jim was doing municipal policing in another location.  He had just dropped his partner off at home and decided to take one last drive by a local used car lot that had been experiencing a lot of recent break-and-enters.  Sure enough, he spotted three males breaking into the cars and stealing the stereo systems.  He was able to capture two of them but the third ran into nearby woods.  Jim got the police dispatcher to call his partner who was by now happily tucked up in bed.  He did arrive shortly after, though.

Jim turned on the PA system of his police vehicle and yelled into it, "Did you bring the dogs?"

His partner, catching on immediately, replied, "Of course," and did an excellent imitation of a vicious dog, howling and barking into the PA.

Within moments, a young boy sporting a Mickey Mouse t-shirt came out of the woods with his hands up, saying, "Please don't send the dogs after me. I give up."

All three were arrested and charged.

The Elliot Shows (a commonly known travelling fair on the east coast of Canada), came to town one spring. Jim and a fellow officer, knowing full well that this kind of event often attracted trouble, made a visit to the sight before opening night. The manager was keen to get one over on the police and suggested that they try out his new ride, The Round-A-Bout. It's definitely not a ride for the faint-hearted. It keeps a person upright at a very high rate of speed by means of centrifugal force. Both officers agreed, determined to be good sports. The owner, however, was not such a good sport. He left them on the dizzying ride, set at full speed, and went off to tend to other business while the two officers got sicker and sicker and lost all equilibrium. Neither were as amused as the owner of the fair.

## CHAPTER FIVE
## THE DARKER SIDE OF POLICING

There is definitely a humorous side to policing and many of Jim's stories are not appropriate for a general audience. It seems to me that without these little moments of levity, a police officer's life would be a very difficult one. The burnout rate for police, in general, is very high and, I, for one, have more than just a little respect for the men and women who put their lives on the line every single time that they put on the uniform.

The dangers are well known. Even officers on the sleepy island of Newfoundland routinely work 12-hour to 18-hour shifts, behind the wheel of their cruisers with very little sleep. It was and is a gruelling routine. Jim was a specially trained arson investigator and often had to travel to other detachments for those particular duties.

The question that often springs to mind when one gets to meet and know an officer is, "Did you ever have the occasion to fire your weapon?"

The answer in Jim's case is a firm. "Yes."

The night in question started off innocuously enough. Jim got a report that a taxi driver had been stopped by a .303 rifle-toting man who proceeded to unload a shot over his head. There were four cars on duty that night, but Jim, alone in his cruiser, took the call. He tracked the man to a nearby church and put his lights on high beam. The man, still toting his rife, stepped out from the shadows at the side of the building. Jim knew him by sight. The man aimed at Jim who immediately used the door of his cruiser for shelter.

John Doe, yelled, "Drop it, Jim."
"You drop it," Jim replied.
"Forget it. I'm going to drop YOU right now."

Jim didn't wait any longer.  As a skilled marksman, he took aim and fired, but slightly over the head of the gunman who dropped his weapon immediately. He then raised his hands in surrender and was immediately cuffed.  Jim was quite prepared to shoot to kill that night as any police officer is trained to do.  It turned out that the rifle didn't even have a firing pin in place but there was no way for Jim to know that at the time.  If the gunman had been killed it would have been considered a "good shoot" firing pin or no firing pin.  The gunman was sentenced to seven years in Her Majesty's service. (Canada is still a member of The Commonwealth and we have a great deal of loyalty to The Queen.  After all, Newfoundland was still a British Colony until 1949.  Those who are jailed often get referred to as being in her service,)

The gunman later said, "Jim, if you'd shot me that night, I wouldn't have blamed you."

Jim's last Newfoundland posting was to the tiny town of Wesleyville.  Before that transfer, however, he was sent there as a fill-in while another officer took a two-week leave.  Before the officer left for his vacation he had seized a cache of weapons from a group of brothers in an adjacent town called Musgrave Harbour.  Unfortunately, this information had not been relayed to Jim.  While on his routine drive through the area later that evening a car came up behind him.  He spotted four men in the car and assumed that they were seeking some kind of assistance.  He couldn't have been more wrong.  No one knows whether they took him to be the other officer or not.  But, from the later-described reputation of these men, it probably wouldn't have mattered.  These brothers had terrorized Musgrave Harbour and the surrounding area for a generation with threats of property damage and bodily harm.  They had all been in jail at one time or another but on this particular night, all were free at once.  They were on a drunken rampage that evening with full intentions to do as much harm as possible.

Jim stopped and exited his vehicle as soon as he noticed they were tailgating him.  Two of the men approached him and the other two circled around and ambushed him from behind.  In the telling, it seems like minutes must have passed but in reality, it took just seconds for them to surround him.  They proceeded to beat him to within an inch of his life.  He was a strong burly man but no match for four well-seasoned ex-cons.  They left him shirtless, beaten, and bleeding in the ditch but Jim will proudly tell you now that he didn't, not even for a moment, relinquish his grip on his weapon.  He hung on for dear life but was too badly injured to get off any shots. He freely admits that if given the opportunity, he would have shot all four until dead. Shortly afterward, a passerby saw his abandoned car with its doors still open. That must have scared off the men. They left shouting that they'd be back to finish him off.

After the detachment was notified a manhunt was launched. Eight squad cars from three towns descended on Musgrave Harbour. A helicopter and a canine unit were brought in from several hundred miles away. It was the most action that the tiny town had ever seen. I imagine the residents, those still around from that time, remember the incident well. The police moved in on the home of the criminals. The four men ordered their dog to attack and they too came out swinging. The police canine unit took the dog down and the men were promptly arrested. All four pleaded guilty and received a sentence of seven years each. Jim was treated in hospital and later released without any lasting injuries. He believes that someone special was watching over him that night.

A few years later when Jim was assigned on a more permanent basis to Wesleyville, he ran into one of the men who didn't even recognize him. Jim had the opportunity to arrest him (gleefully I suspect) for being drunk and disorderly. He was not so brave without his brothers surrounding him. Jim, on the other hand, in my opinion, was very brave to return and work in a town where he nearly lost his life.

A few years ago Jim returned to Newfoundland to visit some of his old haunts. On a visit to Musgrave Harbour, he called upon the home of a man whom we'll call the honorary mayor of the town.

Jim asked, "Do you recognize me, Mr. Smith?"

And he did. After a few moments he replied, "Of course I do, You're the Mountie who saved Musgrave Harbour."

Jim arrived at a new posting on a quiet Saturday afternoon. He'd said his goodbyes to St. John's. His new colleagues took him out to a local nightclub that evening for a "Welcome to Clarenville" drink. Jim was due to start his first shift the following morning. Of all the Mounties present, Jim was the only one who was unmarried. He was instantly targeted by some of the local young women. One, in particular, took his fancy. The feeling was definitely mutual. They spent the evening getting to know each other and made arrangements to meet up again. Jim wanted an early night and so they said their goodbyes. The next morning, Jim, unbelievably, after just leaving the city the day before, was called back to attend an autopsy in St. John's. The journey was a couple of hours long. Arriving at The General Hospital, he mentally prepared himself for what lay ahead. An autopsy is no easy task for any officer. There are a lot of sights that most wish that they could unsee. This one still lingers in his mind though. It was the body of the young lady that he'd met the night before. She and her friend left the club which was located on a busy highway. They were struck by a transport truck. Jim's new friend was killed instantly. Luckily, the passenger survived. He found that autopsy to be one of the most difficult things he'd ever experienced. A young vital woman with whom he'd made an instant connection now lay before him on a slab. The experience stayed with him for many years.

After his final two year posting in Wesleyville and many run-ins with his commanding officer, a meagre salary with little or no overtime pay, and an exorbitant rent, Jim was becoming disillusioned with his life. He missed home and he missed his family. Putting his life on the line every single day for just nine dollars an hour made him feel, understandably, like he wasn't getting anywhere. He was still reeling from a divorce and the loss of his son. Who could blame him for such feelings? He made the life-changing decision to return home to Pictou County. Despite pleadings from many of his commanding officers, one of which flew by helicopter to Wesleyville, Jim turned in his gun and his badge. The pleadings of the officer who flew to talk Jim out of quitting was, incidentally, the officer who had recruited him into the RCMP. Jim felt conflicted, and "between a rock and a hard place" as he puts it. He didn't want to leave the force but felt he couldn't continue in his post with the way things were. The difficult commanding officer was later relieved of his post because of continuing complaints. He freely admits that the RCMP opened many doors for him, taught him invaluable life lessons and enriched his life immeasurably.

His experiences in Newfoundland left him with wonderful memories of the warmth and welcoming nature of the people who lived there. He gained a full and thorough knowledge of the politics and habits of the island folk. It's obvious, through his reflections, that he looks back on his time there with great fondness. He had the opportunity to visit once inhabited ghost towns, abandoned by the residents after the restructuring of the province by the then premier, Joey Smallwood. He, like many Newfoundlanders, viewed this and still do, as a violation of the human rights of the people who were forced to leave their now abandoned coastal settlements. His postings in both Wesleyville and Clarenville also brought him in close proximity to the town of Gander, known then as "The Crossroads of the

World" because of its large and frequently used airport.  Jim spent a lot of his downtime visiting the airport and finally was able to see for himself some of the aircraft that he'd learned so much about during his youth.

I have no doubt that the ROYAL CANADIAN MOUNTED POLICE is a lesser force without his presence.  He still proudly wears the striking ring that he received upon his graduation.  He wears emblemed shirts and jackets and speaks with obvious love and pride of his years with the force. An added bonus was that he could now call himself an Honorary Newfoundlander.

## CHAPTER SIX
## BACK HOME IN PICTOU COUNTY

I think that I'd be lax in not telling you that Jim regretted his hastily made decision to leave the RCMP. At the time of his departure, there was not an officer who would take up the post under the aforementioned commander. If there had been, I'm sure Jim would have quickly risen through the ranks and been with the RCMP until he reached retirement age. Between the two acts – his days as a Mountie and his time as The Raccoon Whisperer lies an entire life.

He was guaranteed a job with the New Glasgow Police Force that fell through shortly after his return home. He spent the next two years going from job to job, including private investigative work. He impatiently waited for an opening in one of the police forces in Pictou County. Pictou County is made up of many small towns, all with their own police forces with the main hub being New Glasgow. Some of the small towns are patrolled by the RCMP. The town lines blur, one into the other, but each proudly proclaims its own identity even though they often run adjacent to each other.

After two years, he finally secured a position with The Stellarton Police Force. Happy to be back in uniform he was just fifteen minutes into his first shift when he found himself staring down the barrel of a gun once more. This time it was a .30/.30 Winchester rifle. It was just a routine matter that brought him once again, face to face with his own demise.

He and his partner spotted a local troublemaker leaving the premises of a known bootlegger. They put on the emergency lights and immediately afterward saw the suspect throwing something from the window of his vehicle. Jim's partner knew the identity of the driver and when he relayed the name to Jim, he recognized it right away. Jim, in fact, had known the man for most of his life. He jumped out of the passenger side of the police cruiser with the intent of making himself known. Unfortunately, because of the waning light the suspect didn't recognize him immediately. His partner wanted to shoot right away when he saw the gun. Jim urged him to wait, then took off his hat to make his face more visible to the man, feeling sure that upon realizing who he was, would not shoot. Jim was armed with a .32 revolver that, unfortunately, had no bullets in it. The small-town police force was fresh out of bullets at the time. Only Jim knew this of course. Because of their past relationship with each other, Jim was able to talk him down and he was immediately arrested. The man spent seven months in federal prison.

From that day to this, the man has never taken another drink. They both met, quite by accident, some thirty years later at a concert. He approached Jim, hand extended in a gesture of apology and gratitude. He told Jim that the incident made him turn his life around and he is now an upstanding citizen and contributing member of his community.

The Stellarton Police Force was a quiet one and Jim found himself doing odd jobs in the office and lots of paperwork – a job that is universally hated by police officers everywhere. After a few years in Stellarton, he was then transferred to The Westville Police Force, back to the town where he grew up.

As a police officer, Jim describes himself as fair but firm. If you were upfront and honest with him, he admittedly would give you the benefit of the doubt. As a man, he describes himself as easy-going, gets along with everybody, which in turn means that he gets taken advantage of from time to time. He's slow to rise to anger but it does happen sometimes. People mistake his easy-going nature and think that he's a pushover. He hasn't won all of the battles that life has thrown at him but he's won enough to be at peace with himself. After spending many hours with Jim, I'm often surprised by his witty comebacks. He has an acute sense of humour that often comes at one at the most surprising times. He often brings his friends to tears of laughter with his great gift of storytelling.

During these days of Covid-19, he spends quite a bit of time in grocery store line-ups buying food for his raccoons. He has a little trick that keeps people at the required six-foot distance. He has a "fart machine" sent to him by a subscriber in British Columbia that he uses with great affect. If someone gets too close he reaches into his pocket, activates the apparatus, shakes one leg, then turns to those behind him and apologizes. He then loudly proclaims that "Wendy's chilli" is most likely to blame for his indiscretion. He is always amazed by how quickly people back away.

Jim's best friend of 62 years, Ronnie, calls him "The Enforcer." Jim proudly tells stories of how he deals with Ronnie's problems, after being taken advantage of by one person or another, or a company that has done him wrong. He and Ronnie met the day after Jim's birthday. He'd received a ZORRO costume from his parents. The costume came complete with cape, hat, mask and sword. It was Jim's pride and joy. While out playing, Ronnie came along and broke off the tip of the sword. The sword was authentic enough with a piece of chalk attached to the end to make a large "Z" on anything he wished to mark, just like the Zorro of TV fame. The broken sword made the 10-year-old Jim sad. While their respective mothers argued over the damage, Jim and Ronnie forged a friendship that has lasted a lifetime. The sword was filed down to half its length and the chalk reinstalled. All was well with Jim's world from then on. His sword was shorter but in return, he had a new best friend.

After leaving The Westville Police Department Jim went to work as a school bus driver. This brings me back to another aspect of Jim's personality. He is a loner at heart, likes being his own boss, and even though he won't admit it, like myself, has a bit of a problem with authority figures. But who of us doesn't to a certain degree? The people who accomplish the most in life and are the happiest, in my humble opinion, are those who dance to the beat of their own drum, reject being told what to do and then seem to go on to do great things. So, in other words, I suppose we can call Jim a bit of a paradox, a personality full of contradictions who likes to work and play alone. He doesn't get bored and if he sees a void in his life then he actively seeks to fill it. He sees life in black and white with very few shades of grey. I believe that he reads people very well, sits back and observes and then makes his own judgement. He would be the man at a party, sitting alone, but not missing a thing that goes on in the room. I know the type because I'm one of these people myself. And yes, people often ignore us or think that were quiet or boring, when in fact, we may be the most observant and thoughtful person in the room.

In light of these facts, it's easy to see why Jim took so well to his job of driving a school bus. It gave him his summers and holidays free with very few people to answer to. He had always enjoyed children and thought that the job would be a good fit for him. And it was. Jim stayed with the job for fifteen years. People very often tell him that he sounds like Bubbles, the eccentric character from the now cult classic, TRAILER PARK BOYS. I suspect it's because people from all over the world are struck by his Nova Scotia accent.  Funnily enough, Bubbles, or Mike Smith, as he's known to those who grew up around him, was a student on his bus for many years. Jim tells that Mike was an extremely quiet boy (definitely a departure from his TV character), who was constantly listening to music while travelling on the bus.  Bubbles was a musician with the band, SANDBOX before he became an actor. His acting debut came about by accident when he was asked to work behind the scene on the set of the show on a temporary basis.  He fell into the character on the very first day.  Many people are fascinated with Jim's Nova Scotia's colloquialisms, mostly only known to us natives.  I think it's a big part of his charm on YouTube.  The only person to ever complain about Jim's raccoons was a neighbour whom he threw off the bus for bad behaviour many years before.  I assume she finally felt she would get the last laugh.  But Jim just went on, ignored her and continued to feed his little buddies.

The last chapter of Jim's working career was with The Empire Company which is the parent company of Sobeys, a large Canadian grocery store chain.  The money they offered far exceeded anything that Jim had ever earned before.  He rose quickly through the ranks and in no time at all he was Manager of Operations.  The new job came with huge responsibilities and very long hours.  He oversaw security and all manner of the day-to-day workings of the large corporation.  He was sent a message one day, perhaps from his parents or someone else that was watching over him from above, in the form of a heart attack.  It turned out to be a minor one that didn't leave any lasting damage.  But he received the message loud and clear. The company awarded him a very generous pension and he then officially retired.

He left behind a varied but interesting career that consisted of adventures that some men can only dream of.  He then made a conscious decision that his retirement was going to be "Jim Time."  He would no longer have to answer to anyone.  He would do the things that he had previously only wished for and live out the rest of his days in Churchville, where he still resides, doing exactly what he wanted to do when he wanted to do them.

CHAPTER SEVEN
JIM, THE MUSIC MAN

As I mentioned before, Jim is a self-taught musician,  He plays every instrument by ear and doesn't even know how to read formal sheet music. This certainly doesn't diminish his capabilities in playing any instrument that he puts his mind to.  He owns four keyboards and an elaborate drum set.  A new keyboard just added to his collection is his pride and joy.  He sings as well, probably much better than most, but not as well as he'd like. In his younger years, he belonged to a few local bands and has now formed another group.  They regularly have jam sessions in each other's homes. The band call themselves SHORT NOTICE.  The income from their gigs goes to assorted organized groups for the benefit of children fighting cancer.

His favourite instrument, the one in which he's most proficient is the keyboard.  This is my opinion but Jim insists that he's more adept on the drums.  His sisters laughingly tell me that during his teen years he drove everybody in the house and neighbourhood a little crazy with his constant practising.  A view that I know is shared by any family who has a drummer living under their roof.  On occasion, he does a song or two for his viewers but when alone, sings at the top of his lungs.

Because of copyright law, when performing another's song, YouTube has to pay royalties to the original songwriter.  Never expecting to be recognized on any level for his music, he was pleasantly surprised to find that he was becoming a bit of a musical sensation when a British woman living in Belgium named Linda Law discovered his videos.  Linda owns several rock radio stations and is a musician in her own right.  She saw some of Jim's videos and contacted him via email.  She interviewed him on her station. He came to her attention when he performed FOOTSTEPS IN THE SAND. They collaborated together on that song, both of them singing from their different locations, with his videos playing in the background.  They have done a total of four videos together and all receive rave reviews from his followers.  Jim receives royalties for his performances as does Linda.   He's happy to have finally made some money from his music even after the songwriters are compensated.

In the early days of Jim's career, while living in Newfoundland as a junior Constable, he was unable to get time off during the summer months. Instead, he would drive a considerable distance to Port Aux Basque, the most westerly part of the province and the location from which the ferry departs for Nova Scotia.  One year, Jim was on a ferry that got stuck in the ice off the coast of Cape Breton Island.  Back in those days, ferries didn't have the capacity to break through the heavy ice floes that come down from the north.  Icebreakers were in high demand because so many coastal boats and ferries were stuck.  March is a particularly bad month for ice in The Cabot Strait.  I can remember seeing people walking over the ice towards Cape Breton rather than remain stranded on the ferry.  There weren't many bunks on board, certainly not enough for every passenger, so walking the ten or so miles, often seemed worth the effort.

Jim's adventure gave him no option but to stay on board because the vessel was too far away from any landmass for a walk.  He was stuck onboard that ferry for a full four days with no icebreaker coming to their rescue.  It turned out to not be such as bad vacation after all.  Because of the time of year, there were very few women or families on board, just truckers.  Jim, no doubt, bored, made his way to the bar where there was a piano.  He got a gig playing for those four days in exchange for free beer.  Food was free to all passengers but they were forced to dip into their own pockets for liquor. After all, what was there to do, whiling away the hours and days waiting to be rescued?  He eventually made it home to Pictou County but with only hours remaining in his vacation, had to hurry back to the ferry in North Sydney.  He was hoping that his commanding officer would take pity on him and give him the extra four days that he was stranded at sea and allow him to spend them with his family.  The officer was not in a particularly generous mood.

"Jim, just think of it this way, you've been on a cruise."

For Jim, music is a way to unwind and relax, an escape if you will, when life gets too stressful.  He sees it as a much better pass time than his flight simulator.  Like most amateur musicians, he plays for the sheer enjoyment of it.

Drawing of the UFO done by Jim right after his sighting in the early morning hours of October 26th, 1978.

Jim's late wife, Jane.

Jim upon graduation from the RCMP Training in Regina, Saskatchewan, Canada.

RCMP Clarenville, Newfoundland 1978

Jim during a television interview with a national affiliate regarding his UFO sighting.

Charlotte and Connor happily together.

Jim being MOBBED BY RACCOONS in the video that went viral and reached many millions of followers.

## CHAPTER EIGHT
## JANE AND HER LEGACY

It was a chance encounter at a laundromat that brought Jim and the love of his life, Jane, together in 2001. They wed shortly after. After all, both had been married before and didn't want to waste a moment of the rest of their lives. Jane had grown children of her own and her mother also lived with them. Jim and his stepchildren got along wonderfully together. Everybody, including her mother, was pleased to see how happy they made each other.

Jane loved animals of every shape and size. She was a soft touch when it came to taking in stray cats and gave both temporary and permanent shelter to ferals. At one point they had ten cats in the house and another sixteen housed in the garage. Their "baby" was a much-loved kitten called Charlie. Jane was the first person in the family to become enraptured by the raccoons. Their first special raccoon was called Rasmis, who had a baby named Rascal. Unfortunately, Rasmis was killed by a car so Jane stepped in to take over the care and feeding of Rascal. Jane tamed Rascal to eat out of her hand. Along came Foxy who would sit on her shoulder while she fed him along with, a now, expanding family. Jim often healed wounds that Rascal and some of the others had inflicted on them by coyotes, fox and other dangers.

Within just a few years, Jane was given the terrible diagnosis of terminal cancer. She sadly succumbed to the disease just a few short years after their marriage. Jim was left bereft. Her dying wish was that Jim continue her mission and feed and care for her raccoons. Their numbers were growing and she didn't want the partially tamed animals to have to go back to fending for themselves in the wild. Of course, he honoured her last wishes and THE RACCOON WHISPERER was born.

As I've mentioned, Jane's mom lived with them and he continued to care for her for another ten years after Jane's passing. They got along well and I think it was her presence in their home that gave Jim a reason to go on. There was never a cross word between them. Jim even gave up his bedroom on the top level of the house and moved to the basement so she could have close proximity to the bathroom.  In the last year of her life, her physical needs were such that Jim could no longer care for her.  She then went to stay with a niece to live out her final days.

Jim's mother-in-law was partially blind.  While Jim was out one day doing errands, he came home to find her nestled on the couch with one of the raccoons.  She had heard scratching at the door and assuming it was one of the cats, let the little animal inside.  It's a story that still entertains to this day. They made quite a sight cuddled together on the couch.

Jim's devotion to his mother-in-law is just one more example of the kindness and love that Jim's followers see in him every day.

Tragically, Jim and Jane's beloved cat, Charlie, passed away shortly after Jane.  It was a huge blow to him.  Charlie was a smart, sweet and loving cat, but more importantly, Charlie was his last connection to Jane.  Charlie was fourteen.  Jim had him cremated and his remains sealed in a beautiful cat-shaped urn that he plans to have buried between him and Jane.  The urn now sits on the cat castle that Jim has in his living room for Connor and Charlotte.  It took a very long time for Jim to recover from Charlie's passing.  Even now, all these years later, his memory still brings tears to his eyes.  I've had cats for all of my adult life.  Some inevitably become more special than others.  They become like our children and sometimes take on the role of loving parents with their instinct to love and protect.  Charlie was just such a cat.

CHAPTER NINE
JIM'S CAT FAMILY

After a while, Jim felt ready for a new family member. Enter Connor Cat. Connor was just two years old when Jim adopted him. He was living a harsh life on the streets of Halifax, Nova Scotia's capital and largest city. A friend came across Connor and thought that perhaps the two would be a good fit. And they were. Connor bore an uncanny resemblance to the much loved Charlie. Connor is a Norwegian Forest Cat, a long-haired black and white beauty. He foraged for food on the streets and I think it's safe to say that he did a lot of dumpster diving. To this day, he has some favourite foods that most house cats would turn their noses up at. He loves Tim Hortons donuts. But no glaze or chocolate, please. He also enjoys French fries and Chinese food, especially honey-garlic spare ribs. Connor had to be nursed back to health before Jim could take him home. He's a tough guy. He was found full of fleas and had a large cyst on his neck that required surgery. He was neutered and then, finally, shaven of his beautiful mane, and brought to his forever home. Connor, despite his years of living on the mean streets, fit in from the word "go." Jim describes his coming with great fondness. He immediately took over the house and made it his own. He was finally king of his own castle. For those of you that don't believe that animals can feel gratitude and relief at being rescued, you couldn't be more wrong. Rescue cats and dogs, in my opinion, make the best pets for this very reason.

If you've watched Jim's videos then you know of their constant battle of the chairs. Jim's recliner became his favourite perch so rather than ousting him, he bought a new one. And you guessed it, that one became Connor's new favourite. He rules the roost. He stays close to Jim, follows him around the house and refuses to allow him to sleep in. If Connor is awake then it's time for Jim to wake up as well. Jim has an aging PT cruiser with a large back window ledge. Connor hears Jim talk about donuts and Connor is immediately at the door waiting for his car ride. Jim recently purchased a new Jeep for winter driving, but, no, Connor is not happy about the new vehicle. He likes the old model better.

There are cats and then there are cats.  Connor is one of the latter, very smart, loving, wily and quick-witted.  He understands what's being said and responds, but only when he's in the mood, of course.  He likes to watch videos of frolicking squirrels and sometimes has a front-row seat to the ones that visit Jim's bird feeders.  After seeing Connor in person, I can attest to the fact that he is as beautiful in person as he is on screen.  He's quite a bit smaller than he looks in the videos.  With his gorgeous black and white coat and dazzling eyes, he's a real beauty.

There are several videos about Connor's escapades, mainly his escapes which number twelve to date and his recaptures/returns.  He's gotten more brave over the years and therefore a little more difficult to find, often taunting Jim from behind a bush, only to run off again when he gets too close.  The lifespan of a house cat is about seven years longer than that of an outdoor cat, even one who has been domesticated.  Jim lives in the country.  The danger of coyotes and other wild animals, ticks, and speeding vehicles make an outdoor existence very risky.  While he's on the missing list, his absence causes not only great concern for Jim, but for his followers as well.  They await his return with bated breath.

At one point, and up until a year ago, Connor was so popular with Jim's followers, that Jim set up a Facebook page for him.  He had 1,500 friends.  People often asked him questions as if he could actually answer.  Eventually, it got to be too much.  Jim could hardly manage his own growing number of followers let alone Connor's so he had no choice but to shut down the page.

Jim felt that Connor may have been in need of a kindred spirit.  Enter, Charlotte.  Charlotte was found in Cole Harbour, a small town near Halifax.  She was about two years old and had a litter of kittens at the time of her capture.  Nova Scotia has a capture and release program for feral cats.  Veterinarians give of their time, free of charge, to cut down on the number of abandoned and displaced cats. Charlotte was spayed and then put into the cat foster care system in the hopes that she would  eventually be placed in a forever home.  After several of these homes, it was obvious that Charlotte was finding it difficult to fit into any of them.  She was offered to Jim.  He took her home but only on the terms that she would have to "click" with Connor.  Just like him, she fit in immediately.  She followed him everywhere, just like Connor did, from room to room and from floor to floor.  Her only stipulation is that she not be picked up.  She comes to Jim on her terms, often lying on his shoulder while he watches television.  She loves to be petted but only feels truly safe around Jim.  She's a typical cat, sweet-natured, but not nearly as smart as Connor. She's a little camera shy and Jim usually has to catch her sleeping so that his followers can see her on camera. Charlotte is a long-haired tabby with a very pretty face. She's settled in wonderfully and came to Jim when Connor had been with him for about six months. She settles for regular cat food and doesn't show any interest in people food.

And finally, there's Smokey The Barn Cat who stays outside or in the barn. There's a debate amongst his followers as to his breed. He's been called everything from a Maine Coon to a Persian and other things in between. He's a large cat, very fluffy and dark grey in colour. He stays aloof, often perched on a tree stump as if surveying his kingdom. With his one bent ear, he can look quite ferocious and intimidating. I suspect that the boldest of coyotes run a mile upon seeing him. Jim suspects that he may have a permanent residence at a nearby farm but probably likes Jim's yard so he can watch the frequent comings and goings in Jim's garden. Smokey never comes closer than the farthest point of the backyard.

Jim so loves his cats, that if one is sleeping peacefully at night on his bed, he will go to another bed so as not to disturb the cat's sleep. That's what one would call true devotion to a pet.

CHAPTER TEN
THE RACCOONS

THE RACCOON WHISPERER was a name given to Jim by one of his followers back in the early years of his videos. Before that, he was just Jim, the guy who fed raccoons. Rascal the offspring of Jim and Jane's first raccoon lived to be thirteen and a half years old. The lifespan of most raccoons in the wild ranges between three to five years old. Obviously, Rascal, their first adoptee, outlived them all. She was very territorial from the beginning and shooed other raccoons away. On the other hand, she frequently adopted orphaned babies and brought them to Jim's doorstep for feeding. Often she came with injured little ones, dropped them off, obviously knowing that he would do whatever he could to heal them. By this time, Jim was able to tell one raccoon from another. He says that it was very clear to him that she was relieved when he took them into his care.

Raccoons are often referred to as "trash bandits." Known for their pointy nose, small dainty ears, and masked faces. They all look alike to most people. But not so to Jim. He considers them to be very wise animals. He knows their various personalities and names many and recognizes them on sight. Sometimes when a hungry stranger comes into the mix he knows immediately that they're not one of the regular crowd. He calls these the feral raccoons, unlike the others who have gotten used to him. But none are strangers for long. After a short time of eating on the run, they too become family members.

Most come to feed on a regular basis and have been doing so since they were babies. They are as used to Jim as they are to their own mothers. There's Bandit, Smokey, Steven Spielberg, who always hides behind the safety of the camera, and Woody, the shy one, Woody most often stands alone, patiently waiting his turn for a morsel. Blackie, Scooter, Sammy, Buddy (who regularly stands on Jim's shoulder nuzzling his ear), Pepper,

Gizmo, Hossy, Junior, (we can only assume that there was a Senior at one time), Bernice and her babies, Grabby, and Casey to name but a few. Jim can have up to 20 and sometimes more in a single evening when the cold weather is starting to move in. I think that because of his shy nature, which always leaves him on the outside looking in, Woody is the fan favourite. There's no doubt that Jim has a soft spot for him as well. The raccoons' jibber-jabber amongst themselves, squabble for Jim's attention, cuddle, but most come to eat, drink and wash.

People from other countries have some misconceptions about our Canadian raccoons. First of all, or raccoons are much fatter out of necessity. In this climate, just like bears, they fatten up as the cold weather draws near so they can hibernate peacefully from approximately December to March. Many of Jim's followers are concerned about rabies. There is no rabies in this part of the world. Sometime, around 2015, a disease called Feline Distemper wiped out about ½ of our raccoon population. The disease mimics rabies in many ways but cannot be transmitted to humans and does not make the raccoons vicious. The only good thing, if one could call it that, is that it results in a quick death, often within a matter of days. Bats, often know to carry rabies have been eliminated from our part of the world too, by a disease called White Mouth.

Jim has never been bitten by a raccoon and he's been feeding them since 1999. Sometimes they will nibble at his ankles to get his attention and he may get a scratch from their almost human-like little fingers. He immediately disinfects and cleanses the wound. He says he gets worse scratches from his cats while playing with them. He never takes any chances with raccoons that he's unfamiliar with and he definitely doesn't want others to think that it's okay to get too close to the little creatures. They are still wild animals, after all, but he is well trained in how to deal with them. He makes sure to always have them view him as the alpha male. Some that he's raised and nursed from babyhood view him as their mother.

The raccoons are never destructive to his property. Sometimes one or two even sneak into the house when he opens the door. They never defecate on his deck, where he feeds them, or anywhere on his property. They respect him enough to do their business in the woods. If one were to corner a raccoon, they will take the easy way out rather than attack. Jim is careful never to show fear even when mobbed by them. He remains the dominant one at all times. Besides, he's the one holding all the cards, or should I say food.

Raccoons are resilient animals. They can survive in the wild on small rodents, berries and are adept fishermen. He supplements their diets and cares for them on a daily basis just as he cares for his cats.

It is against the law in Canada to keep raccoons or any fur-bearing wild animals in the house. He's nursed some abandoned babies in his home, keeps them in a cat carrier, but once strong enough they are immediately sent off to an animal rehabilitation centre.

CHAPTER ELEVEN
THE CARE AND FEEDING OF JIM'S RACCOONS

The first food that Jim ever fed the raccoons was hard-boiled eggs. He then added Hamburger Helper complete with sautéed mushrooms to their diet. Next came peanut butter sandwiches. The crusts had to be cut off for Rascal. She refused to eat them otherwise. Rascal also became a fan of Tim Hortons Honey Crullers. If presented with a plain glazed donut or crusted sandwich she would immediately throw them right back at Jane or Jim. As I mentioned earlier, Rascal lived to be the ripe old age of 13½. She would stand in the yard awaiting the sound of Jim's car turning into the driveway. Jim found her body one day not too far from the house. She passed away peacefully of old age beneath a tree on the edge of Jim's property. He buried her there.

Nowadays, the mainstay of the raccoon's diet consists of dry dog food, Ritz Cracker Cheese Sandwiches, chicken wieners, Vanilla Oreo Cookies, banana bread, unsalted peanuts, dry cereal, and their most favourite treat of all, red grapes. They will eat green ones but most definitely prefer the red variety. It's fascinating to watch the raccoons chomping down on the grapes. They point their noses in the air and chew as fast as they can so they can get a second helping before the others are all eaten. This grape eating is the noise that I mentioned earlier that sounds so much like that of raindrops on a rooftop, the noise that people find so soothing.

Jim takes great care in choosing the raccoon's diet. He avoids additives and preservatives whenever possible and makes sure that their dog food is of the highest quality. It mustn't contain any ash or other fillers. He treats them monthly for worms, removes ticks with a special tool provided to him by Hope For Wildlife, and gives them regular flea treatments. There are always two buckets of water nearby for them to drink from. Some even wash themselves before or after a meal and one of his raccoons insists on washing her sandwiches before eating. People viewing a video of his for the first time worry about the quality of the food that they receive or think that he doesn't provide adequate water. I can assure each and every one of you that their every need is taken care of. If a badly injured animal comes to him with something that is out of his field of expertise he immediately dispatches it to Hope for Wildlife for care and treatment or a quick and peaceful euthanasia.

No one out there need ever worry about Jim, the raccoons, their health or his. This is a man who knows what he's doing. It's remarkable when reading through comments on his videos, just how many are charmed by the cuteness of the little creatures and want to know how to obtain one as a pet. Jim wants to discourage anyone from doing such a thing. Raccoons belong in the wild. Some people may go against his advice but soon live to regret it. Raccoons are foragers by nature, and cute as they may be, could wreck a house in no time by just doing what comes naturally to them.

All the things that he does for his raccoons, of course, costs money. But Jim says that he makes plenty from his YouTube videos to cover the cost of their medical bills and their food. He spends over $2000 a month on his babies. He watches for price cuts on various items that they love and then stocks up. Many of his followers, very generously, want to help out with his costs but Jim wants people to know that their contributions are unnecessary. He manages just fine on his income from YouTube and would rather these generous people give to the local animal shelters in their respective towns or countries.

Jim has made provisions in his will that his house is to go to a relative who will continue to love and care for his furry friends, just as he does.

## CHAPTER TWELVE
## JIM'S OTHER WILDLIFE VISITORS

In Jim's world, no creature is ever denied food. His bird feeders are never empty. The summer brings many species to his back step. In winter, when it's more difficult for the squirrels to find nuts and berries his feeders become their daily hangout. Connor Cat and Charlotte, especially, enjoy the daily squirrel show. Crows visit for brown bread and cracked corn.

In June of 2020, Jim received an unexpected visitor one evening – a small black bear. To my eyes, he didn't seem that small. No bear is ever small to me but Jim called it a teenager. He was bewildered by the lack of raccoons dropping by in the preceding days. When the black bear appeared, he knew why. Raccoons are fodder for predatory animals and they tend to stay well away from dangerous creatures. A few raccoons were brave enough to stay at the bottom of the steps in hopes of getting a few morsels of food but none stayed for long.
The bear got comfy and sat for awhile munching lazily on a few chicken wieners  He was obviously very hungry to venture up onto Jim's patio. Jim watched a while before chasing him away with his booming voice, but not before he was able to photograph the bear for a video. That was his one and only encounter with the animal.

On another occasion, a fox bravely ventured up the steps to grab two Oreo Cookies and a chicken wiener before scurrying off. Jim has also had skunks come to visit and feed. They've never sprayed his step, their gift to him, I suspect, for the food on offer. Occasionally, one of Jim's raccoons gets sprayed by a skunk. Jim has to suffer through the horrible odour until it wears off after a few days.

In winter while the raccoons are hibernating, deer make their way to Jim's backyard. He uses his snowblower to make a path for them from the woods to a circle that he clears for them in the backyard. Their delicate legs are easily broken while trekking through heavy snow so he makes the way easy for them.  Once there, they're rewarded with a feed of deer apples, cracked corn, or multi-grain bread.  Here in Pictou County, deer are a frequent sight in many yards.  During lockdown, they wandered freely throughout the streets and could sometimes be seen peering through people's windows.  I suppose that they thought that the world was theirs once again.  Many farmer's stalls sell deer apples (apples that are imperfect and not fit for sale to the regular customer), for the express purpose of feeding the beautiful creatures.  During times when a heavy layer of snow covers the ground, they can no longer find the berries and leaves that makes up their regular diet.  Jim usually keeps his apples in the barn but when the weather is in danger of freezing the apples he brings them into the house to thaw and then cuts them in half to make for easier eating.  Oftentimes, he buys a better quality apple so the deer don't have to eat bruised or rotten ones.  Hunting deer within the town limits is forbidden by law and there is a specific season for deer hunting in woodland areas.  Jim feels that the only shooting that should be done is with the lens of a camera, a philosophy with which I wholeheartedly agree.  Jim goes through pounds and pounds of apples to feed these graceful creatures and has taken some beautiful photos of them.  I think it's safe to say that Jim is the talk of the forest and if animals communicate with each other then they all know that all paths lead to Jim's back door.  There are three very well-worn paths from the woods to Jim's property, all made by the raccoon's frequent visits.  Jim loves to watch his chubby little babies waddle off down one of the paths to the woods, happy and content after a hearty meal.

CHAPTER THIRTEEN
JIM GIVES

Jim is the recipient of much generosity. He asks nothing of his viewers and pleads with them not to send him donations. That doesn't mean that he doesn't do his own acts of charity. He gives regularly to Hope For Wildlife, the organization that helps him with instructions on how to care for his raccoons.

A few years ago, Jim was presented with four baby raccoons (kits) that had not yet been weaned, They couldn't have been more than a few weeks old and he assumed that their mother had been killed by a car. He brought them into his house and fed them with a syringe every two hours, day and night, until they were old enough to be brought to the people at Hope For Wildlife. No different than a puppy or a kitten one gets attached rather quickly. In one of his videos, they can be seen crawling over him in the hope that he was their mother. He kept them in a cat carrier and after feeding, covered them with a blanket until the next feeding time. This was only one of several times that he nurtured kits from infants. One can assume that some of the raccoons that come to his door these days must be some of those little ones.

Up until a few years ago, he sent birthday cards to many of his followers but now time just doesn't allow for this. If he receives a gift at Christmastime, he is sure to send back one of his calendars. He will, when asked by a relative or friend of an avid follower, give a shout out to a big fan. Recently, he received a request from a young lady to give her grandmother a quick call for a milestone birthday. He was happy to oblige but when the lady answered the phone she said that she'd never even heard of The Raccoon Whisperer. He was baffled but got a good laugh from the incident.

He donates $100 a month to a local cat shelter. The cats at the shelter live in comfort and are free to stay indoors or roam about in their outdoor yard.

The Halifax Regional Municipality has a monthly spay and neuter day. They ask for donations from the public. Whatever the public donates, Jim matches with a donation of his own. He receives hundreds of gift cards, many from the US, that are unusable here in Canada. He promptly passes them on to followers of his that he knows are in need. He has anonymously adopted a local family and makes sure that there is always food on their table and no child of theirs goes without at Christmastime. He's told me of many other gifts to local waitresses, restaurant owners who are struggling during these trying times, and pays for dinners that he's arranged for his friends during the holidays, just because he can. He does much for many. I, too, have been the recipient of his generosity. He recently gifted me one of those special coins produced by The Canadian Mint to recognize his UFO sighting. It's rare and will, no doubt, be quite valuable someday.

I recently interviewed a follower, a resident of Wisconsin, whom we'll call Susan, to protect her privacy. Susan became aware of Jim's videos back in May of 2020. She has some major health issues and struggles to raise a grandson with health issues of his own. His mom, Susan's daughter was murdered some years ago. Susan had recently lost a dear friend and was facing a parole hearing for the man who had murdered her daughter. In other words, she was literally at the end of her rope. Susan made a conscious decision to only watch content that was uplifting and positive in nature. She stumbled upon Jim's videos quite by accident. She was immediately impacted by this delightful but simple man and his contribution to the world of animals. She sent Jim an email to tell him so, but not before slipping five dollars into an envelope to help with the cost of his wieners. Something about her email struck a chord with Jim and he found her number and called her within a few days. They talked for a full hour. In her loneliness and obvious low spirits, she told him of her struggles, holding nothing back. They now talk regularly and she considers him one of her best friends. In her words, "they just clicked." She calls him her phone pen pal. Susan was in possession of an old and failing tablet and was no longer able to send or receive emails. Within days, she received a new Apple iPad in the mail to replace the old one – a gift from Jim. Some months later her car was in need of repair. She needed a reliable vehicle for her frequent medical appointments. The money came to cover the cost of the repairs – another gift from Jim. They have a genuine fondness for each other and now he relies on her wisdom and friendship when he feels overwhelmed. Jim has a great sense of humour that he often keeps well hidden, except in front of those that he knows well but Susan regularly laughs until she cries during their phone conversations. After speaking to Susan, I've no doubt of her sincerity. She feels reluctant, now, to speak of anything that she may need or want for fear that he'll offer further assistance. His impact on her life has been a positive and rewarding one. Through his videos, she's received peace of mind and through their regular phone calls, a new friend. Susan truly believes that Jim has saved her life.

Jim saw a relative struggling with an old and outdated walker. He promptly bought her a new one. I could, without a doubt, go on for a very long time about other acts of kindness that he's bestowed upon others but Jim is reluctant to speak of his benevolence. I believe that what he feels now is privileged to be able to give back, just a little something, to those less fortunate.

One must not forget that Jim is a former police officer and investigator. He is intuitive by nature and an astute judge of character. After all, he's been doing this kind of work for most of his professional life. If he thinks he's being taken advantage of, he has no problem in cutting that person off. There have been scammers trying to collect money on his behalf from animal rescue groups or the like. He's quick to put out immediate disclaimers to his followers so that none are taken advantage of.

CHAPTER FOURTEEN
JIM RECEIVES

To say that Jim is the beneficiary of much by many would be an understatement. He's grateful, beyond measure, for his YouTube success, its financial rewards and the positive impact that he's had on people's lives. He finds it difficult to believe that his following has grown to such heights. When he looks at the number of viewers on a single video reach into the tens of millions, he finds it almost impossible to comprehend. Jim is just an ordinary guy living in an ordinary town in rural Nova Scotia, who's being sought after by TV and radio stations from all over the world. He's had requests from CNN and A&E to participate in documentaries about his life. Inside Edition has recently done a piece on him. It is a surreal experience for him. "Surreal" is an often overused word these days but in this instance, I think it's safe to say that it's the most appropriate one for Jim's almost overnight success. Some days he's so overwhelmed that he just has to check out, turn off his phone, not open his emails and just relax in front of the television.

Gifts of cash flow in from all over the world. Once he received a card from Ireland containing 140 Canadian dollars. It was slipped into an envelope addressed to The Raccoon Whisperer, Pictou County, Nova Scotia, Canada. These days, this information is the only thing that the post office needs to reach Jim. This Christmas he received hundreds of parcels, some of whose postage far outweighs the value of the gifts enclosed. His postal carrier, delivers, always with a smile on her face, bags of Christmas cards. It's not unusual for Jim to open his door in the morning to see a huge box or boxes, bigger than he can carry, waiting for him on his step.

As an avid fan of the Boston Bruins hockey team, his gifts range from stuffed raccoons wearing hockey gear to raccoon face masks for protection against Covid-19. Even though his house has dozens and dozens of toy raccoons, he refuses to part with any of them. To him, fans have thought enough of him to purchase or hand make these items, so they deserve pride of place somewhere in his modest home.

He has hand made afghans, pillows, coffee mugs, coasters, beautifully thrown pottery plates, honouring each raccoon in his family, raccoon toques, framed needlepoint, raccoon t-shirts, jackets, annual planners, raccoon calendars, charcoal and coloured sketches, framed photos of himself and the raccoons, wall hangings and so much more. Just this winter an archaeologist from Oregon sent him, not one, but two battery-operated snow blowers.

A CAA tour guide follower who travels the world sent him a short video of her tours. One of her destinations was Holland. The background showed some cuckoo clocks. Jim, certainly not meaning to throw any hints, told her that he'd always dreamt of owning one. Two weeks later a UPS truck showed up in his driveway with a cuckoo clock.

Connor Cat and Charlotte are never left out. They receive toys and treats from almost everybody that sends a gift to Jim. They also receive Christmas cards, and pictures, and embroideries.

He tries to show and wear everything on his videos that his generous followers have gifted to him. Christmastime shows him wearing a Boston Bruin's Santa hat. But the one gift that he treasures the most comes not in the form of a tangible gift, but one, wholly intangible. It came to him this past Christmas from a YouTube contributor who calls herself Biggi ArtMouse. It's an animated film that pays tribute to Jim and all his furry friends, including Connor Cat and Charlotte. It depicts them all coming together around Jim's dinner table. The animator included all the things that meant the most to Jim including his beloved Woody, outside alone, as he usually is, waiting to be invited inside. It features Jim's musical talents, and more importantly, captures, somehow, because of the animator's skill, Jim's kindness to all. Jim was so grateful that he was brought to tears when viewing it for the first time.

As is often said, "Imitation is the sincerest form of flattery."
Imitators are popping up all over the Internet. Most just leave out some food for the raccoons and then photograph when the raccoons come by to feed. They don't interact with the raccoons as Jim does nor charm one's soul as he does. He's not unhappy about this. He's been trained in how to deal with the animals and doesn't like to see others take unnecessary risks.

There is a trend by some YouTubers to make what are called "reaction videos." These pop up about a makeup artist's evaluation of a newly released brand, or by a DJ's reaction to a song from the past upon hearing it for the first time. Many are being released about Jim. One reaction comes from a popular YouTuber who has over four million followers. This, no doubt, increases Jim's viewership but if people don't enjoy him then they wouldn't be staying with him, and they most definitely do. Numbers don't lie. Most are very flattering. They are amazed by his love of wildlife. Some, though, who have no idea about his rapport with the raccoons think him a little crazy. It's clear that they have only watched one or two of his videos. One YouTuber has a channel, one of the most controversial types of videos, that talks about the huge cheques that he receives because of his videos. They tell of his exorbitant monthly income. Jim responds to these by saying, "If only." Not only are these types of videos intrusive, but they are inaccurate and frankly, nobody's business. He does receive an income from his videos which is more than enough to pay for his raccoon food.

His first cheque, all those years ago, arrived just in time to replace a large portion of his roof that was damaged in a windstorm. His cheques have enabled him to get a badly needed new barn just as the old one was ready to collapse. With his ever-growing number of followers, his paycheque is also growing, allowing him to purchase better camera equipment, a new four-wheel drive to replace his 15-year-old PT Cruiser and a new snow blower. He is grateful for each and every "luxury" that is now afforded to him. But Jim never fails to think about the comfort and safety of his animals and the pleasure of his viewers whenever he makes a new purchase.
But frugal by nature, he still seeks out the best prices for his raccoon food and never misses a sale.

A podcast called KFC in the US has released a video that calls Jim the most giving and wholesome man alive with the most wholesome channel on YouTube. They plead with their viewership to follow him. Their theory is that people want to donate to him because he is the one person who doesn't want donations. An accurate assessment, if ever there was one!

There's a minister in the US who preaches Jim's virtues from the pulpit and encourages his parishioners to follow him. There's a Sunday School teacher who regularly urges her students to do the same. They, and many like them, believe that his kind and giving nature will do all souls a world of good during these challenging times.

A pulmonary specialist that I interviewed, called Doctor D from New Jersey was struggling with anxiety and depression as he was nearing retirement age.  Unsure of what his new purpose in life should be and understandably apprehensive about his future, he came upon Jim's videos and was impressed by this man who seemed so honest and caring about the animals around him.  He became one of Jim's biggest fans and refused to miss a single one.  During a particular period a few years ago, he noticed a marked change in Jim's physical appearance, a change in his mannerisms and a definite wheezing in his breathing.  He and Jim had been communicating via email for some time.  Doctor D immediately reached out to Jim and advised him to seek medical attention as soon as possible.  He was worried about possible congestive heart failure, pneumonia or worse.  He advised Jim as to what tests to ask his family doctor to perform and what medications he thought should be prescribed.  Living over 1,000 miles away obviously made it impossible to treat Jim personally.  Jim informed him that his only medicine at the time was Buckley's Cough Syrup.  Buckley's is a Canadian-made, over -the-counter, rather foul tasting, but very popular cough remedy.  It works on simple coughs but Doctor D was sure that this was something more.  He was definitely alarmed.  It turned out that Jim, indeed, was suffering from a form of pneumonia, and if left untreated, may well have ended with permanent tissue damage to his lungs.

Jim has Type 2 diabetes and has to be vigilant about any health issues.  He credits Doctor D with saving his life.  They've continued their correspondence and have now become the best of friends.  The Doctor, though now officially retired, has been called back to work because of the Covid-19 crisis.  He has gained a great deal from their developing friendship.  Doctor D has now been able to stop taking all medications for his depression and anxiety and is now much more at peace with himself, all because he watches a man every day that he feels is doing God's work and has been touched by his hand.  He finds Jim's videos a great tool to decompress after his busy days in the ICU dealing with life and death situations during this pandemic.

Doctor D takes a holistic approach with his patients and always recommends Jim's videos for relief of stress and as a way for them to relax.  They, too think that Jim is amazing.  The doctor takes great pride in knowing Jim and calling him his friend.  Jim reminds the Doctor of his brother who passed away some 20 years ago, even finding that the two possess some of the same mannerisms.  After the pandemic began he sent Jim regular care packages full of preventative supplies to keep the virus at bay.  He has also sent Jim some wonderful "techie" gadgets that, once upon a time, Jim could only dream of owning.

Jim, as all his viewers know doesn't want donations or gifts yet some make it impossible for him to refuse.  An anonymous source wasn't deterred from leaving 400 pounds of dog food on his back step.  He, almost nightly, dines at a restaurant called Jungle Jim's.  It's part of a Canadian restaurant chain.  He talks about it frequently and viewers are so intrigued that they now want a tour of Jim's favourite haunt.  No doubt, he'll oblige sometime in the near future.  Jim considers the waitresses and owner to be his friends.  Two different viewers from different parts of the world have gone to the trouble of contacting the restaurant's owner to ensure that Jim receives free meals on their behalf.

Another viewer from Australia, who knew that Jim wouldn't take a donation of money for raccoon food arranged for Jim to receive top quality dog food through the local Walmart.  Of course, there was no way that Jim could refuse.  It was paid for in full and waiting for him at the store.  A US Supreme Court Justice sends him a regular supply of raccoon masks that she makes by hand for his protection against the virus.

The intangible gifts are of the utmost importance to Jim but he doesn't want people to think that he's ungrateful for the more material gifts.  He is always amazed at the ingenuity and creativity and the time that people take to make suitable gifts for both himself and his kitties.

There are, also, some unwelcome gifts.  Women send articles of clothing and other questionable paraphernalia.  Some send proposals of marriage and other indecent proposals from themselves or on behalf of their mothers or grandmothers.

No matter what the gift, Jim tries to send them all a postcard or calendar that he has printed for this express purpose.  He wants to acknowledge everyone who has shown kindness to him.

CHAPTER FIFTEEN
A DAY IN THE LIFE OF JIM

Jim dislikes getting up early. Even the pawing from Connor fails to raise him from the coziness of his bed. He's late to bed so this habit is certainly understandable. Since his neighbour has recently acquired some chickens, he's the recipient of fresh eggs on a regular basis. By his own admission, Jim doesn't like to cook. A healthy breakfast is now at his fingertips – a breakfast that he often shares with Connor Cat. I've seen Jim's videos and I've seen him many times in person. Believe me when I say that the camera really does add 10-20 pounds. Jim is much slimmer in real life than he appears on camera. He's still a sturdily built man but not nearly as big as the camera shows. Even Connor and Charlotte are smaller in reality.

Jim enjoys the break that Mother Nature offers him for November to March. During those months, the raccoons are in hibernation and it's just the birds, deer, and squirrels to attend to. He puts out apples and seeds and the animals take it from there.

He has a group of friends – retired police officers and firefighters from all over Pictou County that he gathers with on some mornings at a local coffee shop. Lots of story-telling goes on. One of the frequent attendees calls it "The Liar's Club." Everybody, because of their previous jobs, whether exaggerated or not, have lots of stories to tell.

Jim spends lunchtime and early afternoon chasing the sales at the local grocery stores for raccoon food. The remainder of his afternoon is devoted to his computer – answering the many hundreds of emails that come his way, and the sometimes as many as 350 direct messages on his Facebook account. These days, it's impossible to answer everyone. If there's a comment on one of his videos from a person whom he's helped through a bereavement or cancer treatments then he, more often than not, makes a phone call to see how they're doing. He feels a deep sense of regret that his growing audience makes it impossible to respond to everyone. This responsibility, that he's often unable to follow through on, lies heavily on his shoulders.

Dinner or supper, as we call it in this part of the world, is usually taken at Jungle Jims. After a recent health scare, he's making a conscious effort to eat in a healthier way. He rarely has company and if he does, it's takeout for everybody. He had guests this past New Year's Eve and has frequently had me as a guest for research purposes, but its pretty safe to say that he's most comfortable with just himself and his cats for company.

After supper, comes prep time for the feeding of the raccoons. Sometimes, if need be, especially with the preparation of Hamburger Helper, (his one and only specialty), he gets the food ready for his furry friends. The wieners are usually cut in half (20 pounds at least on a busy evening), the grapes, perhaps up to or more than 10 pounds, taken off their stems, many boxes of cookies and cereal unpackaged and buckets of fresh water dispensed. The feeding usually begins with a spread of dog food laid in rows on the floor of his back deck. Jim sits on a park bench there beside a sign that reads, Jim's Diner (another gift from a grateful viewer). That's the first course, followed usually by the wieners. Cookies and grapes are the final course. Jim has an alarm system set up inside the house to let him know when the raccoons arrive. In the winter, they begin to arrive at about 9:30 or 10:00 pm. In summer the early bird diners often come as early as 5:00 pm. There is the occasional daytime visitor but raccoons are nocturnal creatures by nature. He suspects that they are probably nursing mothers, or raccoons bringing something home to their babies. When nearing hibernation time, he often feeds them up to three times a night. Their "bed lunch" as he calls it, usually cookies or dog food or cereal, can be as late as 3:00 am. Before hibernation time, he can be mobbed by anywhere from twenty to thirty chubby raccoons. The colder the weather, the chubbier they become. Many viewers express disbelief at their size, unaware that they have to live on their body weight for warmth and food for a least four months.

So, now you can see why Jim likes to sleep in on most mornings. Late at night, he's also making calls to friends, made through his videos, who live in different time zones.

Besides all of this, Jim, who doesn't edit or use filters of any kind, most often nightly, records his videos and uploads them to YouTube.

CHAPTER SIXTEEN
JIM'S FOLLOWERS

With the number of followers growing by the thousands every day, Jim sometimes wishes that he could go back to the way things were. It's inevitable that he often feels overwhelmed by the amount of correspondence that he has to deal with every single day. But a few moments given to reading comments from his many subscribers quickly changes his mind. To say that he's had an immeasurable impact on people's lives from all over the world would be a huge understatement. Many are in awe of his giving nature, his unmistakable love for all the creatures under his care, his "down home" uncomplicated charm, and his obvious sense of honour and honesty. The impact felt the most, is by those who are suffering, and just trying to get through the day. I'll tell you some of their comments at the end of the book but it's easy to see that he has literally saved lives.

It's hard for him to believe that his videos have reached every corner of the globe but it hasn't gone to his head in any way. He's the same caring and kind man that he was when he first began his videos all those years ago. He's made friendships that, no doubt, will last him a lifetime.

If for some reason, he hasn't uploaded a video for a week or so, followers will go to any length to find out if he's okay, has fallen or been taken ill. They sometimes track down his neighbours or people who live in his little village, often those whom he hardly knows. These people call from all over the world to have them check on Jim's well-being. Their sleuthing methods astound him but on the other hand, he's deeply moved by their concern. In recent weeks, after his recent health scare, his followers send him well wishes every single day and are as worried about him as if he were a member of their own family.

He has a viewership that includes every province in Canada, and every state in the US. But that's not where it stops. He has watchers from Russia, Poland, Ukraine, all countries of The United Kingdom, South Africa, Turkey, Morocco, Tasmania, South America, New Zealand, and a surprising number of followers from Australia. The list goes on and on. He means different things to different people but I think that it's his pure authenticity that sets him apart and has made him "the talk of Washington State" so one radio station there has reported to him. In Pictou County, his popularity is virtually unknown. It's only in the past few months that he's been stopped on occasion for an autograph. But things are quickly changing. How can they not? From the time that I began this book until today his viewership has grown by at least 100,000 people. He recently received his silver plaque from YouTube for having 100,000 followers. That number has now grown by six times. The next one, in gold, comes with one-million followers. After that is the most special of all, the diamond plaque for five million followers. I have no doubt that he'll be around to receive them all.

Jim's videos calm autistic children and those, both young and old, who suffer from panic attacks and severe anxiety. They are a way for people to tune out from the daily horrors of the state of our world at present. He gets frequent comments from people going through chemotherapy, or from those in the last days of their life or going through a crisis of faith. He helps people who are enduring the torture of losing a spouse or child or a beloved pet. It's only understandable that these people want to give back in some way but Jim refuses to change his stance on donations. He gives people the hope and belief that the world is not such a bad place after all, as long as it has someone like Jim Blackwood in it. Some call him the second coming of Saint Francis of Assisi, the patron saint of birds and animals. He is, indeed, a true Renaissance man.

Jim has visitors from all over the world who email him to arrange a visit to his home just for the privilege of meeting him and to help feed the raccoons. He has of course had TV presenters come to do interviews but there are others who come from long distances to spend a few hours with Jim and the raccoons. They come from Pittsburg, PA, from Boston, MA, from California, from Cyprus, from Korea, and from China. They spend a week or so in a local hotel and visit Jim and the raccoons nightly. One woman brought her mom as a surprise birthday gift. Mom couldn't figure out where she was going when the car began travelling the backroads of Pictou County but the moment that she saw the house, she squealed in delight. She recognized Jim's home immediately. The raccoons, always wary of strangers, flocked around her immediately.  She later told Jim that it was the highlight of her life.

His followers also cross over into the animal kingdom.  There's 34-year-old Louis the Parrot who swivels his head from side to side so as not to miss a trick when the raccoons are on screen.  There's George the Goose who's owner features George on his own YouTube channel.  There's a miniature pot-bellied pig from Wisconsin who is equally transfixed when the raccoons come on,  and then there's the charming videos of Charity the Cat, a beautiful little kitty, who remains still, eyes glued to the screen throughout his videos and then wants more.  Sweetie, another adorable kitty is also a big fan.

Popularity on YouTube is not without its pitfalls.  There are the so-called keyboard warriors, who behind the safety of a computer screen, feel that they have the right to use the platform to bully, make inappropriate comments and intimidate.  Commonly known as trolls, these people have no problem being as mean as they can be, uncaring about the effect that they can have on the people on the other side of the screen.  In his early days of filming, upon receiving some of these nasty comments, Jim quit the platform for several days.  His feelings were deeply hurt but he eventually decided that they were not worth his concern.  Nowadays, Jim has a total of thirteen monitors and a video manager, (two Canadians and eleven Americans) who work tirelessly to sift out the mean comments and do so without compensation of any kind, just for the privilege of working with him.  Quite an homage to the man, don't you think?  Any comments left on his message board containing words such as "please stop," "fat," and "rabies," are deleted.  Of course, they also weed out profanity of any kind.  They also answer as many questions as possible that don't require Jim's personal attention.

Jim has acquired a stalker or two over the last few years.  Stalkers can be dangerous and unpredictable, even though they often declare their undying love to the object of their affections.  If they find themselves blocked or ignored, they will often do whatever it takes to get even.  But this, too, is one of the prices paid for fame.

Jim once received a call from The Department of Fish and Game in Alaska informing him that what he was doing with the raccoons, was in fact, breaking the law.  They continued on in a similar vein about rabies and other dangers that these wild animals could present.  He listened patiently for a while but then broke in, "Do you folks up there in Alaska have internet access?"

"Yes sir, of course we do."

"Then I suggest that you Google Nova Scotia. It will be clear to you then, that Nova Scotia has absolutely nothing to do with Alaska, or indeed, with The United States of America." He hung up at this point but still gets a chuckle out of the story to this day.

On another occasion, The Canadian Department of Natural Resources appeared on his doorstep. Jim was able to tell them more about the habits of raccoons than they knew. He is the expert, after all! They found that all was well, that no raccoons were actually living in his house, which is against the law in Canada, and then passed him a piece of paper, and quickly left. There was nothing more that they could do or say and no citations were given. Jim was doing absolutely nothing wrong.

Very recently, the actress, Diane Keaton, reposted one of his videos to her Instagram stories. She's not the first famous person who has taken a shine to his channel. Sharon Stone has posted his videos on Instagram. Both recommend watching Jim.

CHAPTER SEVENTEEN
JIM AND YOUTUBE

He, unfortunately, has recently had a scammer on Instagram going by the name of, THE_RACCOON_WHISPERER (note the underscores that Jim does not use). This imposter has set up a PayPal account and is asking for donations to help with the care and feeding of his raccoons. Jim is deeply disturbed by this and wants his followers to know that this person is a fraud. He's reported the person daily and has asked his viewers to do the same. His biggest fear is that some of his loyal followers, especially those who can barely afford to, send this person their hard-earned money. It is definitely one of the perils that anyone on social media has to deal with, but something that none of us can seem to avoid. Vigilance is the only solution. There are people from all over the world who make this their life's work and earn millions committing cyber-crimes.

YouTube is very protective of Jim and they take every opportunity to put his videos on millions of people's feeds. His ads make money for them and with his rapidly growing fans, they are keen to do anything that they can to support him. Ads appear on most of Jim's videos. If a person doesn't watch the full advertisement and presses the skip button then Jim does not receive any financial compensation for that view. The more views that he has, the more that Jim can profit, thereby one can donate by just watching and viewing the ads in their entirety. They are usually no more than 12 seconds long.

The story of Jim Blackwood speaks for itself. I feel no further need to sing his praises. They are obvious to all who know him personally and to all who have come to know him through his videos. He's the real deal. I'll conclude, though, with words from just a few of his loyal followers. They say it all so much better than I ever could.

"I love the fact that people like this man exist."

—K Brah

In Nepal, the villagers here call him "Kin Tan Tee" which means, "Nobel man who is loved by many animals... who, in kind, he loveth too."

—EB

"I've been smiling for ten minutes,  This is so wholesome."

—Aceeiprt

"This is wholesomeness overload.  You have a pure heart."

—Unknown Entity

"God bless you!  I wish you a long and healthy life and we need more people in the world like you."

—Lis Perlata

"This is a happy man with a heart of pure gold. Absolutely amazing.  May he live a long and peaceful life."

—Daria Timothy

"This is the Disney Princess that we didn't want but the one that we needed."

—Bonnycrybaby

"He reminds me of my Daddy in heaven.  God bless The Raccoon Whisperer."

—Cindy Brewster

"You are awesome dude.  Thanks for being so wholesome."

—Micah Mars

"I wish there were more people in the world like you."

—Maria

"Connor Cat is the coolest cat in town."

—Peter VanDemark

"You are my favourite man on YouTube.  Part of my daily routine."

—Allen Love

"One of the few places you can go to relax and smile."
—Anthony U

"Sir, believe me when I say, the longer your videos are, the more therapeutic they are. I enjoy watching your daily comings and goings and the various raccoons and the bits and pieces of your life, like your friends. It takes me away from my own problems, if only for a little while. You are feeding the raccoons, but you're mentally feeding the rest of us."

—John Doe of France

"I thought something was wrong. Haven't seen you for a while. Glad to see all you guys are healthy and happy."

—Colleen Chevallier

"After the stress of the day, I come here to lower my blood pressure and reclaim my humanity."

—Right Indignation

"I swear these videos make me feel like I'm visiting my grandparents."

—Lunis night

"There are watchers who suffer from PTSD, depression, some with severe depression. Others are bed-ridden. Some are dealing with loss, or they have a serious health diagnosis. This is a safe place where they can rest their weary minds and torn out hearts for a time and feel good again."

—Wren Wrenwood

"I Love how the raccoons run down to your car when you get home."

—Tara Lown

"To all the trolls out there, these videos bring much joy to my life. Don't try and ruin it or you will have me to answer to."

—Edwina Caparelli

"You really are a sweet man and your work restores my faith in humanity. Thank you for all that you do and for the entertainment. God Bless you!"

—Jennifer Toussant

"You are loved all over the world. You deserve an Honorary Doctorate from your local university."

—Robyn Forman

"I have only one wish in my old age, and that would be to come to your house and meet you and visit. I couldn't imagine anything better."

—James

"My heart is melting, this is so precious."

—Beth McCraken

"Isn't God wonderful! He made us such lovely animals to love when we feel lonely and depressed. Just watching these wildlife babies makes us feel happy and loved. And the man who takes care of them, I think the Good Lord is smiling at him. Just like we are when we watch this man."

—Deb Russell

"I just have months to live but I know that you've probably prolonged my life because you give me so much happiness. I know heaven will be full of people just like you."

—Anon

"You are Canada's go-to pandemic show. Fun family entertainment."

—Jeffrey Skinner

"I hope you realize how important you and your furry friends are to so many of us alone at this time."

—Janice Lawrence

"Your energy is so needed in this world right now. Blessings to you and your pets."     —Child of God

"My 12-year-old autistic boy is enthralled with your videos. It calms him down like nothing we've ever tried before. He is soothed to sleep by your fur babies."

—Anon

"This is my nightly dose of serotonin. Thank you Mr. Blackwood."

—Donna Williams

"James Blackwood, the man the legend, the conversationalist."

—Ginger Wright

"Good evening from England. James, do keep up the fantastic and inspirational things that you do."

—Richard Keough

The above quotes are taken from some of Jim's videos over the years.
Thank you to each and every one of you for your contribution.

# ACKNOWLEDGEMENTS

I am absolutely indebted to Jim Blackwood, THE RACCOON WHISPERER, himself. Without his candour and unwavering trust in me, this book would not have been possible. Always available at a moment's notice, I'm truly grateful for his cooperation.

I must thank Gary for his gentle support, advice, love, encouragement and continued faith that I could complete this project even when I thought that I could not. He is responsible for introducing me to Jim and his videos. He recognized, even before I did, that his story should be told.

Thank you too, to my Beta Readers, Sandra Dunn and Wendy Littlejohn. An extra special thank you to Sandra for her editing skills. With a friend and mentor like Sandra, I already feel like this book is a "winner." From the very beginning, you loved what you read, wanted more, and inspired me to keep moving forward.

Much thanks goes out to Dr. Jaz Robbins, M.A. AMFT of Pepperdine University for her beautiful tribute to Jim in The Forward of this book and to Susan of Wisconsin, and to Doctor D of New Jersey for their openness and willingness to be interviewed.

For my cover designs and printing, thank you to Eastern Sign Print and staff.

Last but not least, thank you to my webmaster extrodanaire, Rob Parsons of Parsons Designs.

To my son, Daniel MacKinnon, Creative Consultant/ Manager/ Best Son Ever for all his research and advice, loads of love and thanks.

To my present and future readers, where would I be without you? Stay in touch regarding future projects by checking out my website regularly at christinemackinnon.ca. You'll find all my social media links there.

You can also email me at cmackinnonauthor@gmail.com.

# BIOGRAPHY

Born and educated in Newfoundland, Canada, Christine now resides in Nova Scotia. Her works have been published in several anthologies and magazines and she is also the author of her memoir, CHRONICLES FROM THE HALL, available on AMAZON.

Made in the USA
Las Vegas, NV
08 June 2021